Help Me Understand

What Happens When My Pet Dies?

Kathleen A. Klatte

PowerKiDS press™

NEW YORK

Published in 2020 by The Rosen Publishing Group, Inc.
29 East 21st Street, New York, NY 10010

First Edition

Editor: Rachel Gintner
Book Design: Rachel Rising

Photo Credits: Cover Uberphotos/E+/Getty Images; pp. 4, 21 LightField Studios/Shutterstock.com; p. 5 Eric Isselee/Shutterstock.com; p. 6 eurobanks/Shutterstock.com; p. 7 VP Photo Studio/Shutterstock.com; pp. 9, 11 Pressmaster/Shutterstock.com; p.12 Alohaflaminggo/Shutterstock/com; p.13 fizkes/Shutterstock.com; p. 14 Boris15/Shutterstock.com; p. 15 Jeffrey M. Frank/Shutterstock.com; p. 17 wavebreakmedia/Shutterstock.com; p. 19 Bulltus_casso/Shutterstock.com; p. 22 ESB Professional/Shutterstock.com.

Cataloging-in-Publication Data

Names: Klatte, Kathleen A.
Title: What happens when my pet dies? / Kathleen A. Klatte.
Description: New York : PowerKids Press, 2020. | Series: Help me understand | Includes glossary and index.
Identifiers: ISBN 9781725309586 (pbk.) | ISBN 9781725309609 (library bound) | ISBN 9781725309593 (6 pack)
Subjects: LCSH: Pets–Death–Juvenile literature. | Pets–Death–Psychological aspects–Juvenile literature.
Classification: LCC SF411.47 K53 2020 | DDC 636–dc23

Manufactured in the United States of America

CPSIA Compliance Information: Batch #CWPK20. For Further Information contact Rosen Publishing, New York, New York at 1-800-237-9932.

Contents

The Circle of Life

One of the best things in life is having a pet. Pets such as dogs and cats can play with you when you're happy and cuddle with you when you're sad or tired. Smaller pets can be fun to watch and talk to.

Sadly, no matter how well you take care of your pet, like all living things, pets **eventually** die. Your pet may be old or sick or get in an **accident**. Or they simply may be a kind of animal that doesn't live very long.

Many kinds of animals make great pets. They each find a special place in our hearts.

Why Did My Pet Die?

Doctors who care for pets are called veterinarians, or vets. They go to school for up to nine years to learn how to take care of different kinds of animals. Many times, vets can help hurt or sick animals. Sometimes, though, they can't.

Sometimes, animals die of old age. Dogs, cats, and some birds can live ten to fifteen years or more. Smaller animals such as fish and hamsters might live for less than five years.

veterinarian →

This little boy is keeping his dog company while the vet treats the dog's **injury**. Some injuries are easy to treat. Other illnesses or injuries may require a **specialist**.

7

What's Best for My Pet?

Sometimes, a pet is too sick or badly injured for the vet to make them better. Your parents, together with the vet, may decide that the kindest thing to do is to end your pet's life gently. This is called euthanasia (yew-thuh-NAY-shuh).

That's a scary idea, and it's OK if it makes you feel sad or upset. Just remember, animals don't understand that long or painful **medical** treatments might make them feel better later. They just understand that they're sick or hurt right now.

Everyone wants what's best for your pet. Your vet will explain things so your family can make the best choices for all of you.

→

What Will Happen Next?

First, the vet will give your pet some drugs to make them very sleepy. This is so they won't be scared or in pain. You'll have some time to say goodbye to your pet. When your family is ready, the vet will give your pet another kind of drug that will help them pass away. It's very quick, and your pet won't feel anything. They'll seem to just fall asleep.

It's sad to say goodbye to your pet, but now they're not in pain anymore.

Not everyone can stay and say goodbye to their pet. It can be a very hard thing to do.

Sad, Mad, and Scared

When your pet dies, you'll have a lot of strong feelings. You'll probably be very sad and want to cry. You may also feel angry if your pet's death seems to be someone's fault. You may feel **guilty** for things you did or didn't do for your pet.

All of these feelings are natural. There's no right or wrong way to feel. Just be sure to talk to a trusted adult who can help you understand what you're feeling.

It hurts to lose an animal friend, but your parents will help you. They're feeling sad now, too.

13

What Happens to My Pet Now?

After your pet dies, your family may choose to bury its body. Depending on what kind of pet you had and where you live, you might bury your pet in your yard or at a pet **cemetery**.

Your family might choose to have your pet's body cremated. This means that your pet's body is placed in a special machine that turns the body into ash. The ash is then returned to your family in a container called an urn.

pet urn

Hartsdale Pet Cemetery in Hartsdale, New York, is the oldest operating pet cemetery in the world. It's been open since 1896.

Saying Goodbye

It hurts when you lose someone you love very much, whether it's a person or a pet. Remembering how much you loved your pet and all the fun you had together can help make you feel better.

Your family can hold a **funeral** for your pet. You might share your favorite stories or make a special photo album. Your parents might also help you pick out some supplies to donate, or give, to an **animal shelter** in your pet's memory.

Your family might plant a tree or some flowers in your pet's favorite spot. You can also pick out a pretty statue or put your pet's name on a small garden stone.

$\longrightarrow$

17

I Miss My Pet!

You might miss your pet more than you miss some people who have died. There's a good reason for that. Your pet lived with you, and you saw them every single day. They might have slept with you at night. It's only natural that you miss them more than someone you didn't see very often.

You might especially miss your pet at the times of day when you fed them or took care of them.

Seeing your pet's things will make you sad for a while, but it does get better. Just remember to tell an adult how you're feeling and ask for help (and hugs!).

19

Comforting Thoughts

No one knows what happens after a pet dies. Some people believe that pets go to heaven. Others believe that our pets wait for us at a place called the Rainbow Bridge.

It might make you feel better to remember your pet's time with you. You can look at pictures or videos of your pet and remember how much fun you had together. It also helps to share happy stories about your pet with friends and family.

A special photo album is a nice way to remember your pet. Some animal hospitals also make clay copies of your pet's paw print for you to keep.

Someday

You may feel sad about your pet for a long time, but eventually, you will feel better. Nothing can ever replace a pet you loved, because each one is very special.

Some people miss their pet so much that they want another one right away. Others need more time to heal. It's OK to tell your parents what you're feeling. Someday, you may find that there's room in your heart and in your home for a new pet.

Glossary

accident: An unexpected and sometimes bad event.

animal shelter: A place that provides food and housing to animals in need.

cemetery: A place where dead bodies are buried.

eventually: At a later time.

funeral: A special service held for someone who has died.

guilty: Feeling that you have done something wrong.

injury: Something that hurts you.

medical: Having to do with the practice of medicine, or treating illness or injury.

specialist: A doctor who deals with health problems related to a certain area.

Index

Websites

Due to the changing nature of Internet links, PowerKids Press has developed an online list of websites related to the subject of this book. This site is updated regularly. Please use this link to access the list: www.powerkidslinks.com/HMU/pet